FINISHING LINE PRESS
www.finishinglinepress.com

WHAT SWEETNESS FROM SALT

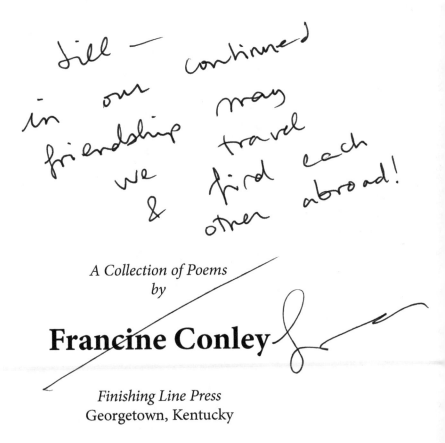

Jill —
in our continued
friendship may
we travel
& find each
other abroad!

A Collection of Poems
by

Francine Conley

Finishing Line Press
Georgetown, Kentucky

WHAT SWEETNESS FROM SALT

Publisher: Leah Maines
Editor: Christen Kincaid
Cover Art: Sean Patrick Hill
Author Photo: Malin Lövkvist
Cover Design: Elizabeth Maines McCleavy

Printed in the USA on acid-free paper.
Order online: www.finishinglinepress.com
            also available on amazon.com

Author inquiries and mail orders:
Finishing Line Press
P. O. Box 1626
Georgetown, Kentucky 40324
U. S. A.

Table of Contents

For Frank

What have I made
but an ocean in you
from my skin?

EVE'S DILEMMA

—based on *Adam* and *Eve*, ca. 1510 (anonymous)

Suppose the garden mound upon which she stumbled stunned
as a revenant was smut. Suppose the glass window through which

I saw myself as a passenger in a car that sped along the lake's rocky
shore was smudged. Suppose like Eve I couldn't discern where

we were headed, but the night convinced because it was dark and
without stars. Sorrow wailed from our speakers, or maybe ecstasy.

Suppose it was our hunger that made me think of her as I reached
inside a bag and offered what my fingers found by feeling: a tiny

apple; a gift we rolled back and forth between our cupped hands,
your bite overlapped with mine as the sweetness of taste diminished.

Suppose the teeth marks you left in my skin by a fire that same night
were those on the apple Eve dared. Maybe the blithe look on her face

was the languished one I felt in me after we devoured what we could.
Eve's dilemma is not simple. She sees what she wants; wonders how

far to reach into the thicket for a damn red spec ensnared by leaves
made greener by distance. Should she keen? Should she wonder how

every little thing that grows in us lies under the sun? Like her, I know
ruin. I know when the apple slipped from our hands, we bit into more

than fruit; that the taste of a story changes in time; can be reduced
to a memory buzzing with flies. Suppose the apple was rotten before

our first bite. Suppose Eve didn't understand the order of loss—or her
own sweetness—and that insects love the infection of sugar. Suppose

the story starts here: with the core we tossed out the window and into
a night that swallowed the stray seed that grows inside Eve like a riot.

Stray

I was born open-
mouthed.

My mother called me
fat girl

the year my father took
so many plump lovers

we lost count.
She measured each one

against the diet
she pared down

to ½ English muffin a day.
After breakfast,

she'd quit the table,
announce: I'm going

to walk the dog.
We didn't own a dog.

So with her hand
holding an imaginary leash

my mother withdrew
into the budding hollow

of our yard. Summers,
our windows half-

open, I listened to her
vomit into a bush,

though bush made me
think of vaginas,

like eating made
my mother imagine

my father fucking
women she never

saw. After heaving
she snaked her way

back to the porch and
called out to a stray cat.

Her bony fingers
tickled the air

as she yelled in a shrill
German accent:

Here Pussy!
Come, Pussy!

I pressed my face
against the screen

and watched her,
body winnowed

to a sickle, lean over
the purring one, who,

yes, always came back.
Such a nice pussy…

By then my father
served me seconds

or thirds. (You give her
too much! she said.)

I swallowed all of it.

The day the stray
vanished, my mother

asked—in confidence—
if my father killed

her. No, I replied,
looking at him:

Pussy left. She
was starving.

The Cells

—After Louise Bourgeois' installation series, "The Cells" (1991)

There is a missing in me that never leaves.

A home with rooms like cells, wire walls, gaps, and beyond:
these spaces: a father, mother, someone else
I forget.

There is the room in which I never lived or slept.

The house light never flooded;
the one I thought I lived, but didn't.
Always peering out of window panes, waiting for

a return. When left alone in my room
all sounds cast a panorama.

I was hidden—an apparition to neighbors
who spied on me from slatted blinds.

I became a shadow pacing between frames.

If they were home we sat at a table and ate in silence.

I watched their mouths move, swallow up
the last patches of food.

I never spoke.

Hours, days went by as words burrowed deeper
into my throat, but my eyes stayed open.

I listened wildly.

Then, just once—I heard it.
An engine sputter: a car wending its way down the sinewy street,
and the exultant withdrawal. It was nothing
but headlights turning onto a drive,
but what to make of the sudden rush

to erase all signs of waiting
for them to return?

They were ruthless about absence.

If I cried I was told I exaggerate the scars.

"You need to learn how to be alone."

*

Tonight, a cold white light startles me awake.

The engine fades.

I run to my room like a cell and crouch in a bed weighed down by covers.

The room verifies its shadows were always there.

I was never alone; I let nothing in.

Not waiting; not hiding.

I imagine what it is like for others.

I hear a key flesh its way into the door.

I close up like a tulip.

I think this bed is enough to protect from what they will do.

I think it will save me to pretend I am asleep.

Salt

What could I wring from salt, what sweetness, say,
from the anchovies I was forced to stomach as a child.
You eat what's on your plate whether you want to or not.
Say we eat what we refuse. Say I go to Rome.
You can go there, Rome, you can go to choke like I did.
So worried about my son swallowing a bone
I stifled on a sharp bit that wedged in my throat
like a nail. The doctor said gargle with salt water
to loosen the speck. Then he jammed a tool inside
my mouth to seek a thing already gone. It will feel like
it's still there but really, there's nothing. Say
you apply this to other parts, like my father, and
his body, all that business he did with women
other than my mother, bodies I saw collapse into
his arms like the one naked as battle and ready for him
to enter her like a cannon when bitch rang from my throat.
He pushed the word back in my mouth with soap,
stood behind me and I studied his nakedness
in the bathroom mirror, soap against my tongue,
foam dripping down my cheeks and into the sink.
Say a word like bitch and you'll be cleaned out. So. Say
bitch. No. Say idiot sorrow. Say it like I said it again
and again for my mother who always wanted to know
more. Say I lied about what I saw and gave her
what I could invent: strands of hair, ripped panty
hose, pools of cum that smelled like salt. Say I lied
because it held her attention on me. In time bitch
stuck in my throat like a bone. Stayed like salt
on my tongue. I used to think it tasted different
in every country. In Switzerland salt tasted thin,
almost sweet. In Germany; like cake. In the Czech
Republic, like coal; in Italy, rugged and in France,
lavender. Now a man writes, I see you as a wild woman
who likes being alone. I won't tell him all the places
I've run, the clinging I've done to the living salty ones
I should add here with a feature or two: the one
with a body like a broken stamen, eyes the color of

branches at twilight—or the man who never says much
let alone love even after I pronounced it. Love is
speaking too much salt. I have traveled far
as the lesser parrots that flock cedar trees in Rome's
Borghese park. Their blue eyes and bionic green tails
punish the sky with color. I stand beneath them;
gargle briny sounds back and forth while deep inside
a room somewhere else in Rome my son wakes from
a dream, asks if the bone is still in my throat. When
I say no he wonders if swordfish swim in oceans or
lakes; if there is such a thing as sword sharks that saw
through water, and how, if thirsty, do they drink salt.
Go back to dreaming, I say, but he won't until I promise
to relinquish the answers. Okay, I will, I tell him,
tomorrow I'll explain everything: and we'll cook
together, we'll invent something new: a wild,
unbelievable taste, and before I finish he adds:
promise we make it with nothing but water and salt.

The Blue Fountain Sings

After De Chirico's "The Poet's Pleasures" (1916)

In the painting the orange glow lifts
the otherwise flat piazza into the air, set against
a cerulean dream, a cloud of steam bursts from
a train passing in the extreme. Close up,
shadows turn, lean. Unbearable arson
heat—thick, huddled. A clock tells time
but the buildings look deserted; shaded
archways beckon: come closer still. Hide in here
with me. The blue fountain sings. Something
is still alive. I could go on forever like him,
the blanched figure that strays, as if retracing
his steps or walking into the first light.
I lost my way there once. The orange path
stretches on without us knowing why.
       If you want something too much,
give it away, my father said. So I left him,
a red stool, some old stone, then traveled
realms of orange. *Hey! You remind me
of someone else I know!* a man yells into
my ear at a club where beats strobe
lights before we wake up in a bed
and cannot find a way out. He calls
me by another name. Oh! To have
a face that sings so blue, to be a woman
like a train passing through. I cannot
stop. And I have nothing left to show,
no other face than this. So look: now go.

The Destruction of the Mother

—After Louise Bourgeois' "The Destruction of the Father." (1974)
and Paolo Uccello's "The Virgin and the Child" (c. 1440)

I am alone in my room when
I receive a postcard of Uccello's "Virgin

and Child." On the back, a scrawled note
in the best of my mother's voice: *I am sorry*

to hear things have been "a little tough." We're at
the beach. I am well—so are the dogs.

*

In Dublin's National Gallery I search
for the painting. I flew here to see
the Virgin take hold of the Child.

*

When I was young my mother brought me
to see Louise Bourgeois' "the Destruction

of the Father," a sculpture that tells a story
of her own father and his ongoing affair

with the family's nanny. In a small case
egg silhouettes rest on a bed. Bourgeois

loved plaster and latex because she could
cast liquid and let it harden into shapes:

a bed or a table, a table like a bed. Like
the bedroom I snuck in to watch my father

and his lovers sleep, thinking, *I see you.*
We make love, are born and die in a bed,

says Louise Bourgeois. She found a frame
for suffering in a table. I think less of

the father and more of the one missing;
the mother who although absent receives

the love of the father, gives birth to a child
she would rather not hold and another

she wants to hold but who wants nothing
of her, and a third who dies before she can

name it. I don't believe in childhood,
my mother said to me once.

*

We are walking along the shoreline,
my ears beholden to the ocean,

the reliable sequence of waves
when my mother asks without asking:

I have not heard from my son in a year.
I must not reply directly for it's not of him

but the world she cares more to know:
the urge to dump waste, ditch, and slight

living creatures. She is most at ease
near the ocean, though troubled by dunes

and their diminishing. *People are killing this
world!* She shrieks, pointing to banks

overcome by the swell: flotsam-dotted sand,
her streaked hair flailing in the wind,

body kneeled to prayer as she hefts steaming
puds of dog shit into recycled blue bags.

*

At dinner, we were obedient,
but I thought it was droll,
as a child, to be called "the
children." Possessives are vulgar,
she added. What are we going
to do with the *children*?

*

Later, she bought a third dog
and named her *Bella Donna*
to replace the woman
my father left her for
or the child she miscarried
soon after.

*

On the beach I study her crooked profile
set against the dunes, three limp leashes in hand,
stranded jellyfish, bulbous shapes
in the sand that recall Louise Bourgeois.

Ocean foam swirls around our ankles.

I don't know in a few weeks
I too will miscarry a baby inside me
before I leave her for good.

Come here, Bella! she shouts in a voice
swallowed by winds, but Bella
doesn't obey.

Damn dog.

*

I do not pretend to know this mother.

*

When I find Uccello,
the plaque reads: *A Motionless Madonna.*
But the Child looks as if she wants to leap out
of the frame—or the mother wants
to throw her child into the arms
of any observer.

*

There is almost no beach left.

Where sands were plentiful there is now a gulch.
I want to start a letter: *Dear so and so,*
no doubt things are *a little tough,*
the casual horror of dunes.

*

It's nonsense, really, this Virgin and Child.

And now that she and I are perfectly apart
I imagine her dogs as the happiest in the world,
trampling on dwindled dunes, residual grasses,
their slapdash paws gone adrift,
coated in mud.

The ocean is swelling whether we want it
or not—and when it's all eroded—when there's nothing
natural left—people will talk,
wildly, about destruction,
about the beauty of a mother undone.

An Old Woman Cooking Eggs

—After Diego Velasquez (1618)

What is she waiting for?
A wooden spoon rests in her lean hand,

an uncracked egg cradled in the other.
In the terracotta bowl: two yellow yolks

glint like cat's eyes. She looks at the boy
who glanced at her before his attention

strayed. What has he done?
Palpable shadows swallow the unsaid,

their faces lit by an unseen fire, a glow
angled such that the burning must be me.

What would he tell me if I asked?
He chokes a flask of wine in one hand,

but adores an orange gourd
in his other arm, imagined desire.

The silence he wears is mine, a thick
furrowed brow. I want to kiss his lips

stained pink underneath. What to do
with the rest? A leaning brass pot,

porcelain bowl, and squeezed
between: a bright knife sharpened

to cut a red onion I missed, there,
waiting to be noticed: tufted roots

knotted to its head, so focused
and fused it is every lover

I've ignored.   I go back again.
Have I dreamed it there?

It's not the boy I need to taste,
but the onion's living purple skin,

until my lips, like memory,
are stung alive.

A Natural History

"Authorities say a boy has been arrested overnight for allegedly breaking
into Paris' Museum of Natural History and cutting off a tusk from
a centuries-old elephant skeleton with a chainsaw."
—March 31, 2013 CBS News

Because some want to owe nothing to the world; because it wasn't enough
      to let it all decompose—an African elephant: a gift
from the Portuguese to Sun King Louis XIV in 1668; because it lived thirteen
      years at Versailles a royal menagerie star died, embalmed
and propped as a skeleton in a necropolis of other precious fossils—tusks
      removed and replaced with look-alikes
to stave off thieves; because three-hundred and forty-five years later a neighbor
      woke from a bad flu bout
in which he hallucinated a blade aimed at the bridge of his nose snapped,
      into the silver sound of a real chainsaw
and parted his curtains to the silhouette of a body inside the dim bone-
      filled museum—red hat, bright white sparks
like gnats swarming the shadows of his cheekbones; because it was 3 a.m.
      the neighbor dialed the cops
who held the phone at a distance from their flaccid ears and tried to take his
      pleas to "save the elephant!" seriously—tried
not to laugh into the receiver as the Chief with chubby fingers waved two
      cops arguing over a chess move
to siren through rue Buffon and find the boy still in the act, enthralled; because
      the saw's high-pitched cry
drowned their clanging keys and footsteps approaching from behind;
      because of the glinted blade—
the boy's white as straightjacket arms gripped and nothing on his mind
      but the pills
snug in the pocket of a hawker dawdling the pillars outside Gare du Nord
      a few blocks from the squat
where his pals still lie about where they come from, birth names
      irretrievable as the print on newspapers
folded beneath their skinny calves; because they wait for him to come home;
      because he loves the chainsaw's weight
and vibration in his hands but the cops' heat shocks in time to toss the tool
      at their feet and bolt through the same window
he broke into—same squashed evergreen hedge, same dusty gravel paths
      he sped through once paved for *flâneurs*

to behold fauna and flora in the 1795 *Jardin des Plantes* zoo where Rilke
        strolled, stopped, studied a Panther
and wrote: "his vision, from the constantly passing bars has grown so weary
        that it cannot hold anything else;"
because the boy sees the thousand bars as an opening to a mighty will,
        panther long gone, a grizzly asleep,
a sloth clinging to a branch—only a gray wolf awake circles his worn path
        in a defunct cage at the zoo's eastern edge;
because the wolf pauses, lifts his snout and takes in currents carrying
        the boy's sweat—sweet, sour,
speckled fear—because the zoo hasn't changed since 1871 when *Communards*
        in one last gasp occupied the zoo
in hopes France could be reborn into a new nation but unable to stop
        Prussian and French troupes
ordered soldiers to starve resistors into capitulation; because
        they didn't give up and out of hunger
ate every zoo animal in sight; because for years after the Bloody Week
        cages stayed empty and the paths
fell into disrepair though a few passers-by swore beyond the tainted bars
        they saw a cramped panther pacing
alone; because the boy never learned legends of his own city nor
        of those who fled before him
he doesn't notice the light flash in the wolf's eyes who stalks his climb up
        the wall near *Quai Saint Bernard*—
on the ledge: to jump or not—tusk slung over his shoulder, still warm
        from the blade's heat, the alarms bleating
into a jaundiced sky; *voleur*! its lineage in escape, wings, thief;
        because he couldn't stop running
until now, where he stands, the world catching up to him—cars streaming
        along the *périphérique*—
the Seine's mellifluous surface—its dead and drowned reflect nothing,
        everything; because the boy so entranced
by lights thinks he's nothing except what he can do next so he jumps,
        and as he lands on the ground,
fractures one ankle, tries to get up and go on with a part of the tusk
        on his back but he can't; no: he can't walk
so he collapses and trembles into a memory: waiting for his father

to return but he never did; because he waited
and read himself to sleep each night his mother sunk deeper into grief huddled
     beneath a kitchen table sobbing herself
into a folded heap as she lay next to the sink—apron stained with sauce
     burning to a crisp in the cast iron skillet—
purple flame lit—faucet open and hot   water running; because he left her
     there, never shut off the water,
the sounds of a city outside the open window becoming a river
     in which he never learned to swim;
steam fills the room and devours her to vapor: yes: because he thinks his mother
     was unmade of her bones; because
the cops crowd around him now and ask who he is and what he is doing there
     and how did he get a hold of that tusk set beside him
like an accident; because he doesn't know what to say so first says nothing
     the way I say nothing to a childless friend
who never smelled the rank odor of a boy's skin after he's been running
     all day from who knows what enemy real
or imagined, never smelled fear on a kid like the one sprawled on the sidewalk
     his cuffed hands behind his back—eyes wet,
gleaming; because when I ask her "did you hear the wonderful story
     of the elephant tusk?" and she responds, No:
there's no wonder left in the world; dumbass thought it was ivory—Because
     as she says this I open the door to my son's bedroom—
his naked body sprawled in white sheets; because he is twenty like the thief
     tipping into manhood I check if he sleeps
in a locked or panicked position; because he is home after a string of bad luck
     he yells his father's name
in nightmares in which I imagine he looks into a long hallway when his father
     leaves us worried his son
would fall into the same pit he did at his age: hording bottles of booze behind
     the same rank pipes pumping
the same tainted water into the same washer that cleaned his vomit stains
     off our shirts; because my son
is already known for stealing knick-knacks from any open window, has lied
     about the color of the sky
and the old woman seated on the park bench so charmed by his question about
     what she sees above didn't notice him pilfer

the engraved locket from her half-open purse—like he didn't notice
        that she names the wonder
in the sky's frame she admires cerulean, a word he might learn to alternate
        with blue; because I wonder
how my own son could become so unrecognizable but I suspect his father
        told him the world is nothing:
you will never amount to anything: you'll be just like the rest; because his father
        told him that too and the story goes on:
a natural history museum is built to store fossils and bones so we can talk
        about evolution; because I tell my son
you owe the world but don't believe that much is true; because the one sitting
        behind bars never heard about his birth:
how his mother passed out; how he crowned into the hands of a nurse
        and found nothing, no nipple's liquid gold
waiting for his lips—though Louis XIV claimed gold his purpose—loved it
        so much he threaded it into costumes
he was barely able to walk they were so heavy, laden; he even had gold paint
        sprayed over his naked limbs
before he danced in front of his mother in the gardens in which
        the Mammoth Elephant strolled boredom
into thirteen years; because some argue Louis suffered from maternal lack
        and expressed it in architectural
plenitude; because the gilded droplets my son's tongue relished from my nipples
        was not enough, as if seconds into the world
it was all up to him and not to this mother or the mother of this thief
        who was gone before she saw his face;
because of this I am awake: it's 3 a.m. in the U.S. and I want to go back
        to the Natural History Museum
where my childhood began: to those rooms my schoolmates and I scoured
        hand-written signs we read aloud
to each other, rummaging the ossuary dictionary for Latinate roots—
        osseus, vena, nervus, cartilaginem;
because our ears and eyes took it all in, uniforms soaking skeletal must
        I want to owe nothing to the world
but wonder, give it back to the one who thought all that was left for him to do
        was hustle a chainsaw
from Clignancourt's *marché aux puces* and go to the museum he knew he could

break into, rooms he remembered
from his childhood full of fossils and tusk, as if he could get away with it,
        forgetting someone is always awake,
always paying attention, especially when a chainsaw is involved, and it was
        then, only when startled
by the jangle of a cop's keys and the word *voleur* that the boy woke
        to the world's limits and started running
to save his life, running fast, then faster, as if nobody is going to catch him.

Ariadne Abandoned

—After Titian's "Bacchus and Ariadne" (1534)

Is it the semi-precious stone-blue Lapis-lazuli
that draws the eye in? Or is it Bacchus' foot floating
there in the frame, as if running into air, struck by
the arrow's relief, the first sight of Ariadne:
a kite string longing, please come flying?
This moment they meet—on Naxos,
lust-at-first-sight—burns in the eaves of my mind
as I see how above them grows a blue choir riot,
and below: dubious browns, barbaric greens.
We meet Ariadne abandoned after she helped
hurry Theseus from the labyrinth—and how
he leaves her standing on the edge, alone,
waves rolling, his ship hissing off in the distance,
the long vein of departure.
She is ruined, incoherent, the Minotaur
still primal but then Bacchus leaps like light
into the electric air, and as if a child he counts
to ten and tells her hide or seek what she is
missing. Forget the betrayal of labyrinths!
Watch me! he seems to say, watch me draw joy
from these trees, plants and rin-tin-tin of revelers!
Near him, two cheetahs yank a chariot, a dog
growls, a man wrestles a snake, another bears
a heavy wine cask on his back. The mouths
are still warm from the taste of a slaughtered
calf bleeding red on their tongues.
We are all hungry for love. Given
a choice some of us will eat the feast raw.
Even the satyr stands center and looks directly
at me, beckoning, as if to say: go in deep.
So Bacchus ascends and reaches, pulling her
from the moving beasts. But what can save me
from the inaudible loss memory cannot hide?
I remember the clutter in my first
lover's gaze, all the frightened birds inside
my mind, the awkward love we made under
an intolerably high ceiling speckled with glow

in the dark stars. For years I was no one
until like Ariadne abandoned I was taken,
wasted by vows, and whatever I owned
gone. Alone I learned to bargain stone
for stone—Lapis, Amber, Jade.

       But see now how Bacchus takes her
crown and throws it up into the air, the heart's
release, a circle of spinning stars, their luminous
clamor—a constellation named Corona—
how it floats there in the loud blue glare,
a brightening above her head!

Pillow Talk

"I want to wake up with you." —Anonymous

The first time we try to make love
he turns on the TV, says he needs it

not to think. Over his hairy shoulders
a documentary flashes violence in Uganda,

child soldiers hired to kill their own.
He climbs on top, stops, unrolls a condom,

penis gone flaccid so he pumps it up
as I watch ghost-green kid-soldiers

ransack huts, slay a village, slice cattle
red, shoot into smoke. Dust shadows

of mothers are shoved to the ground—
rapes blurred, though screams close-up,

jump cuts to pleading palms, wailing mouths.
(It's all on mute.) He says he needs to love

this way since he quit drinking. *Television
is my glass of wine, my version of escape.*

When he comes I swallow bourbon inside
my burning mind. He wheezes, stiff weight

on my hips, fingers in search of a slim
he slinks out of the package, sets between

his lips like a prayer, smoke coiling rings
from the O of his mouth, dissolving. I am

dissolving into this: I am disappearing.
Promise you'll do that to me, I think, but don't

say. I want to be smoked like a Hollywood
cigarette. He gazes long at the ceiling,

starts his brand of Pillow Talk, musing
affectionately on the percentage of Irish

American migrants, victims of the famine
like his ancestors—30% being a more

accurate count, he wagers—regarding
the number of unskilled laborers

exiled in the US, and how it's still *greatly
exaggerated.* I shudder. *It was a terrible fate,*

he exhales, chortling how his Great Irish
Uncle Bart held such high hopes but only

made it as far as Bethlehem, Pennsylvania,
before so drunk he keeled over and died

in the snow. All in the genes, he snorts,
and by now we're both laughing, while

beyond, soldier boys glitter sweat. Dark
glasses subtract their eyes; cameras hawk

every move they make: empty bottles of
gin hark the air, rifles aimed skyward like

Brancusi's gilded birds. As we lie in our
unmade bed kids smear blood on their lips

and kiss the camera lens. They must never
sleep, I say, then change the topic: I'd like

a kid of my own someday, since my clock is
ticking... As I say this remote ash lands

in my eye. He's not listening. He's already
under the sheets, a migrant tongue working

hard to find what's missing inside me.
I hear my mother in my head: *men are shit,*

so I try and focus on taking my own
pleasure. In between takes he gasps

for breath, sneezes, glances at the TV,
takes one long, last drag, flicks the stub

into a cup of coffee. It sizzles
into a silence like mine as he eyes

the wound between my legs, cum
coating his stubble in a nuanced gleam.

The Wedding Portrait

—After Van Eyck's "The Arnolfini Wedding Portrait" (1434)

In the painting the couple stands with their hands
touching and enough apart to notice the shaggy gray dog
smiling between them. The woman's shoes set on the floor
next to the man are shackles. The bed is a burgundy field,
her shadow thrown against it, waiting to be grazed.
A mirror on the wall stands between them, catching
what? Everyone talks about the mirror; how perfectly
it holds our attention, how novel to imagine oneself
seeing and being seen by the painting and beyond.
Others mention the lush emerald dress she wears,
how the plump and folded front makes her look pregnant.
But she is waiting to be done. She is not holding anything
inside her. What you might miss is the window, barely there,
how it beckons inward and outward and how the rectangular
hint of sky it dares emit is enough to leave one wanting more:
more lit cobalt refracting pleasures beyond, more sounds
of children playing in a market below, the day thriving
despite them. There are a few oranges that linger mute
as fruit on a table just below the window, and there is one
on the sill, that rests alone. The orange of its skin
nearly glowing, absorbing the ray of light allowed in,
as if want finds its place between two opposites.
What does it feel like to be them? Sufferers of
delay, what lives between the orange and window
but a desire to be used and useful? This thought is
unbearable to the one looking, who wants as much.
But what else would there be in seeing and being seen
except to endure and enjoy refusal—this not-enough
light—this quashing of succulence, joy withholding
joy—so long as it is kept from vanishing?

The Blue Window

When reason sleeps the sirens sing. – Max Ernst

There is the room.
There is a window in the poorly lit
room, a table. In the air
the smell of a conversation
about guns—pistols,
rifles, bazookas.
Such an old thing, hope,
like a roach on the wall.
There are three places to sit.
A war somewhere near.
Three chairs, a crooked, old table,
a blue window that looks
onto every little thing. Curtains
parted enough to let in a crescent
moon. The child put to bed,
husband gone too. An empty
chair, but an old woman awake,
seated, smoking in the dim.
The blue window lets something in.
Nothing to see but the wasted face
of one who looks at the crescent
moon, eternal, the way its light
peers into every crooked thing.
Such an old scene. And
the way she looks so blue.
Where are the other two?
Their chairs remain, plates too.
There is never enough room.

The Kitchen

"A wise woman puts a grain of sugar into everything she says to a man,
and takes a grain of salt with everything he says to her."
–Helen Rowland

They showed me how to finger wild carrot blunts,
snip flowered kale leaves, tear the terse from sturdier
stems. The kitchens I knew were womanless; full

of men who cooked, silently, mouths riven enough
to sample sauce or graze. I snuck in, helped them
cut, trim, heft handfuls of severed greens into bowls

covered and ready to simmer. Shaved frozen
butter into flour, a few splashes of water, careful
not to knead too much or you'll kill it, then

rimmed wily sides of pans with flattened dough
stabbed by a fork so the apples could breathe
sugar. I peeled and stripped knots of ginger,

gleaned scallions, sliced them into thin rings
stuck to each other. Stout, bolder onions startled
tears that filmed and blurred everything I saw.

I guarded myself cutting meat, for how I sliced
through a thumb once. There was the bled wound
a man mended with the same fat needle and thread

he used to stitch a turkey. Nights were bottomless,
boiling pots of water; days: pans seared with oil,
peppers sautéed crimson. Years honeyed into

turnip torment; the past a splash of vinegar
that worried beets from plum to sanguine,
potatoes yellowed into curry, anise clumps.

To cook with men was to learn how to season
the world into something we'd consume, and we
did. Quickly. I loved the exquisite, pinioned forms

of their hostile hands, scarred fingers that pinched
saffron, gripped iron skillets scorched with living.
I tasted everything. There was one who handled

lit flames and fired garlic into chords of music I'd
never forget. A mound of ripe tomatoes we stacked
into a tower leaning crimson, on the verge of falling.

Greenland

"According to Inuit culture in Greenland, a person possesses six or seven
souls. The souls take the form of tiny people scattered throughout the body."
—Annie Dillard

Small islands drift below *I'll never go there* and Look the Norwegian
          seated next to me on the plane says *Swollen* the moon he means is
full and alive as the snow below hazy as powdered sugar melts on my tongue

We are flying overseas I am a fireman the Norwegian says to me
          flexing his biceps and *Down there* he adds *She skis Greenland*
his English so broken I am not sure if he dropped her there or wants

to forget her like the burning rooms he enters but his lips are opal
          are full he takes my hand and pulls me toward the window we look out
and I am inside the night Michael and I ran through snow deep in

a forest where the moon set between branches made the night not black
          but indigo I couldn't keep pace the drifts locked my knees
but Michael was a gazelle so fast he leaped and reached the cabin first

still running looked back laughed his mouth open wide as ecstasy and
          flew straight into a glass door that shattered
he turned into shards sliced into his body his face like a snow flake

glitters though one big shard shivered so deep into his bicep a round
          blue muscle fell out steaming into the cup of his
hand so when I reached him the snow at his feet went red the world

went red shafts of light from inside the cabin lit the dog who watched
          from the window as we looked at each other and said nothing
and Michael calmly put the living thing back into the slit of his arm

the way the sky calmly puts the sun inside itself each night the way
          Michael who came out and was disowned by his family
calmly put himself back into death last week I heard he cut into his

wrists and was found alone in sheets soaked red a note said who am I
          when I am not wearing my body but that night we ran
his insides spilled out of him and he was not afraid and in time I lost

touch or do I mean I never touched him I just left him like an island
there is no way to hold everyone together no way to put
a life back into the world once it leaves us afloat Michael I am finally

flying over Greenland but it is gone I mean it is *not close enough to touch*
I think as the Norwegian leans in his muscles safely contained
inside his skin and asks me knowing *What is it you are so afraid of living*

Sugar

Split doesn't come close. There is beauty in not
knowing. After, I saw a blue sky firmly parsed

by clouds. But the sky is not a language: the sky is
beyond. *You'll never find someone to love you like that,*

my mother replied over the phone after she heard
me say split. I heard water running near, thought

it was a river, but it was just a faucet, her fingers
fluttering in dish water. She was looking out her

window, at the sky, counting the plates she scrubbed
clean. Nothing but water filling wires when she said:

you got what you wanted: now you're alone. Live with it.
Like an electric jolt—*alone*—and a mangy pigeon

lands in my mind, stalks for crumbs. Feather-torn,
gimp strut, he wrestles chunks of taffy strewn

from a bag of dropped treats. *Dirty! Bad!* yells
the mother as her boy chases, grasps the pigeon

until he sees candy, seizes the scattered bits
covered in muck. He looks up at her yelling,

his green eyes wet, then mouths handfuls of soiled
pink gob, sucks, slurps, and all I can do is watch.

He knows it must be in there: succulence. And
the mother—she grabs his mouth, spears two fingers

inside, scrapes his throat raw, makes him gag
and spit the rest. Once I mouthed *cunt*

and my mother scolded: *to taste such a dirty word!*
then undid my lips, stuck her bony fingers in deep

and scrubbed until I too gagged, my tongue forced
out of me the way a newborn splits from the break

between a mother's split legs, latex gloves pulling
out the rest, each new tear stitched over the old scar

such that I can no longer say *split* but I can still
taste how faint sugar stays inside the smallest

cavities of the boy's teeth: stays long after she scrubs
him clean, long after my mother has scrubbed

each dish into a singular brilliance, long after
she's done looking at the sky outside her window.

Before I called, I practiced how to say split with
no inflection. Does what we say come out how

we want? Like now: I say *split* again and again
until alone I am nothing but a dirty old mouth.

The Bat Situation

I drive away.

Just you and me, Mom.

My son does not turn to look at his father
leaving us, his body haunting into the outline
of a rearview.

*

A blue crayon picture of a valley——a mother
—hurried, scribbled hair—
a boy—boomerang smile.

Fire beneath them—they are floating,
gliding into a yellow awe.

But what about the rough black strokes
that cross the sky?

*

When my father left us
my mother drank her nightly glass of wine
and cast longer glances at the back door.

It was not through thresholds I imagined
his return but through the endless
fractures of plaster cracks on my white ceiling,
webbed lines like an x-ray
of tiny broken bones.

*

At a New Year's Eve warehouse
art party the clock rings midnight.

I kiss a man with a mustache.
There is no difference
between old and
new husbands.

My lips are parted,
body unsuited in a crowd
of costumes,
artists who take pictures
of themselves
with a trick camera
while above us techno
beats blue-red-blue-red.

                    *

After he left my mother replays her loss
through mine and decides we must see

Yves Klein's blue women so we go and
watch a looped silent film that documents

the making of his blue paintings, naked
women who squirm while groups of men

in suits smoke and watch and point and
smoke and watch and point and clustered

firemen in hats aim hoses at them and spray
down their untouchable skin douse them

head to toe in paint until smeared so blue
their white teeth flash and blue breasts bob

these untouchables slip fall slither women
so laughably blue their limbs are fractured

wings flapping dumb against a white canvas
ground made to be a sky as if they are birds

dying blue into white or drowning in depths
of blue they writhe in paint hair tangled

as seaweed they stumble spin and Yves
he just glides back and forth dodging

blue spray his lithe bony fingers with nails
sharp as claws clutch his cigarette

as he would the outcome of each canvas
unknown as the ash of his cigarette burning

down to nothing inside his mouth it is all
burning down—

                    *

I spy a bat in a panic-white tub,
wings tucked beneath
his brown furred belly—
delicate feet, long bony fingers.

How did he get in here?

He must have heard me
enter the apartment,
maybe thrashed against the walls
until his heart seized mid-air,
or he dropped to his death
for no other reason
than he couldn't go on
not clutched to something.

                    *

Because he does not understand
the word dream, my son says,

his eyes almost closed: *wait for me
to leave.* To dream is to leave,

which means I must stay.
Stay with him: stay until he sleeps

so deeply he doesn't notice me
leave. *I will never leave you,*

even when I'm gone. The room
holds the song of our breathing,

and deeper inside our walls,
bats cluster.

   *

My bat situation, I say, to Herman,
the landlord, referring to the problem
I need fixed.

The sound of each letter spreads over my tongue
the way as a child I watched my father,
a painter, stretch white canvas taut
over each hammered wooden frame.

   *

After I tell her about the dead bat
found in my tub at midnight

George yells "Right on! Bats
are shamanistic signs of rebirth!"

She pulls me outside to smoke,
curse; offers a sip of whiskey from

a jam jar hidden inside a paper
bag, promises not to cry

since she is not in love
and it's another new year.

*

A bat's skeleton is the framework
for wings. "They're dumb fliers,"
mutters Herman. "Your bat

must have snuck through cracks in
the floor," he goes on, pointing
downward with a shaking index,

"or some odd fault." His hands
tremble the way my father's did
when he searched for beads

or small toy bits I pretended to lose
in my room. Once my father crouched
and stuck three fingers into a crevice

along the floor, yanking a red
ribbon I'd funneled into a hole
on purpose. Then shook as if

splintered but he was crying—
tears like insects on his face. *Dad?*
She's leaving me! he gasped.

*

Too drunk and swooned
by music George mistakes

the window for a door—
shrieks, *Hey! how the hell*

do you get back in that hole?
Fuck it! she slurs,
twisting her body and
pulling me through

the frame: *No Risk:*
No Rapture!

         *

"Inside these walls is dampness
so dark it's only fit for bats.

There must be colonies living
and dying inside your room."

Herman grins as he says this,
looking straight through me.

         *

This is how we move: our hands caress the walls
the way my father smoothed each canvas before
he painted nudes.

I spot a fracture in the wall but don't tell Herman.
I wait for him to find it: think: *go ahead and fill it.*

He winks.

         *

My phone rings: it's him:
I want to come back.

*

I am done with blue.

I don't trust Yves Klein.
Don't trust a man who left
and calls from an overseas
island where cold means

negative blue. Nothing to do
for these nameless faceless
blue women all but dead
and gone and hung in cove

after cove, outlines filling space.
There must be one who begs:
stay, wait for me to leave.
Then I find her—in another

room—not blue
but Melancholia, gray
and black, Dürer's engraving
unsuited against the wall's

vast white sheen, supplicant
of loss, sulked and
surrounded by keys, a globe—
She sits, a downcast

gaze washing the ground,
counting the missing.
She ignores the bat
hovering above her.

The inscription claims bat,
darkness, and woman
as allegory: *Melancholia is
the world.* Or maybe it says
something else—my sight
is failing.

*

George is kissing a woman
with blood lips
at the heart of the pit
she is Ecstatic
Melancholia
she is Music
the World
she is Darkness
and everything
I want to forget.

—*Look!*

She stops, eyes me
from the heart of
the throbbing,
her lit blue cheeks
smeared in lipstick.
I — Am — Here
I mouth, slowly,
pointing
to the wall
behind her,
where a bat grins,
its eyes alive,
absolute fire.

Refinement

It's indecent to hope after so much loss,
like the day when from between my legs
blood ghosted out and what I thought
was alive in me died. I leaned on the sink,
watched as a baby emerged in unspoken
clumps. My son, building Legos
in the other room, heard me gasp:
Mom?—I answered, my voice
an ironed shirt, telling him: *Just tidy up
your toys.* As he played on I grabbed
towels to clean up the mess, but couldn't
keep pace with the flow, wringing blood
over blood into the sink, watching it all
drain. I wiped, mopped the vague shape of
a hand on the floor, tossed it in the toilet,
flushed. Nothing could contain
what terrified out of me in shapes
so voluminous and stringy, so I gave up,
drove to the ER, son buckled in back,
rags wedged beneath me as more bits
emptied out in waves. Once there
the EMT joked I had good plumbing,
told my son not to worry, his mother
would survive, then, looking at me, added:
a woman knows what to chuck and what
to keep. That hour turned into years, and
now that I'm alone and done with babies
everyday I lift my body out of bed less
and less refined. Even my stomach
shows no trace, though for weeks after
I looked pregnant enough for strangers
to stop and ask when I was due. *Fuck off,*
I replied, thinking I ought to speak
with more care so the dead in my body
would not flutter of out of me like this,
sounding so pitiful, until the day
an old woman came up and said, *honey,*

I've been where you are: soon you'll
come back to yourself—it's just
your body thinks there's still life inside,
and it will keep on believing the lie
until the day it's ready for the truth.

Bees

For the Hive

Those were years I told one man after another *sure,*
I'd fuck a lug like you, why not. I looked down the barrel

of each rifled gaze because I wanted less to be like a woman
who waits than a man who takes as he pleases, enters a bar,

surveys the perennial variety, chooses which one he'll take
home. No longing; no loneliness allowed: just action.

I screwed inside the frame of a deflated waterbed like a ship-
wrecked coffin. In a forest near Fowl Bay where bent over

a felled oak I heard termites gnaw marrow as a Meditator
quoted Thich Nhat Hanh holding my ass from behind.

One so short I leaned wheelbarrow-low and threw out
my back. A full beard at a pit stop in Manitoba who cited

his trophies and bowling techniques before the white walls
dotted with red tulips bounced to the drunk beat of our bang,

one plush stomach against another. I will never apologize
for lust, I said, to men who asked. To me sex was less sacred

than ponderous, from the verb *ponder,* meaning to weigh
and, distantly, *egg.* In time each shag scored was less

a victory over gender than a weird, fragile exchange
in which I was given an egg to hold, or so I imagined,

as if to warm another vulnerability inside mine without
breaking. One yowled he'd never touched a woman,

only men, and when I whispered I didn't care, he fainted.
I told the firefighter who cried in my arms ecstasy is not

the end; it's when we go beyond and, for a second, are not
ourselves. He said, sorry, that sex without love was, to him,

the wet burnt smell of a forest days after its been doused.
But what if it isn't about love after all; what if sex for me

then was a way to give shape to the untailored cloth
of crude truths I witnessed as a kid in a father and others

after? I wasn't always careful: I dragged outrage feet first
onto the sidewalk after he tried harm. Even his egg has

a name. There were gems, cock-kickers, mopes, punks.
There was fast talker, divorced and with kids who bellowed

Yeats' "I will arise and go now, and go to Innisfree,"
when I told him the job was done. Then a slew of brooders

like sapphire with their beautiful, busted faces, the lanky one
who sculpted what he called my ruined feet as we lay on

the floor of a rented storefront, leaves blowing through
a mail slot. That was less raunch than letting night seduce

dawn, the warp and weft, woven skin feeling skin on hands
on skin. Later, a poet who leaped over the bed like a flying

squirrel, citing Groucho Marks. Somewhere sloped near
the end of my safari, I grew tired of my body's hollow mess

when on a bus to Chicago I sat next to Eriks, a painter
who added an "s" to his name for pluralizing purposes.

I was going to an installation on taxidermy, animals
my long-distance lover stuffed and posed before TV sets

he left on static. "Music emanates from the gaze of dead
beasts," he fretted, "especially horses: because when eyes

can't shut they don't lie." But no one keeps eyes open
during orgasm, I argued, as we humped under a grizzly

he'd nailed to a wooden platform on wheels. We rolled
around the studio, pumping toward our own little deaths,

when his way of looking at me started to make me feel
taxidermic. Eriks listened to the story, frowned, upset not

at the details but the 20 blocks I'd go alone to find this one
he guessed refused to meet me halfway. When we arrived

in Chi-town, he invited me to share a bowl of warm soup
at Bumblebee Diner. As we entered, the place glowed in

that legally blind way—outlaw yellow booths striped black
and white. Eriks asked one question after another, as if

clearing cobwebs from the basement windows of my psyche,
then pointed to a mirage on my arm, an unfinished tattoo

by one who yelped giddy-up! cum time. Eriks didn't flinch
when I told him what I experienced as a child. He set his

spoon down, and in the time it took our soup to go cold
he wrapped his hands around mine like a canoe and stared

into me. It was hard to brace against his gaze, but the longer
he explored my face the more the fictions I worked so hard

to armor myself with were stripped. There is no escape.
I am as you are, he said, his face turning into broad lowlands,

big sky view. The world cleaved at Bumblebee, and I was
alive. After he walked me where I'd meant to head, he touched

my cheek in a way that transformed me from the inside.
I could hover with you a really long time, he finished, then turned,

leaving me at the door of the one I'd come so far to sleep
with. As he slipped away a cascade of smells and an electric

field of flowers appeared in my mind, a motley of bees
doing their fantastic dance, swarming aster to lavender,

golden rod, sunflower, helicopter-close to stamen, pistil,
and petal. Laden with as much pollen as she can hold,

the worker drones back to the hive, a smudge of truthiness
lost after so much sex with flowers. On her return, chalky

and sweet flavors she swallowed swill into a cocktail she vomits
onto a waxy canvas. She fans her heap dry with furious,

beaten wings till it's a honeyed, edible shape, then goes on
for the sake of the hive, her life a solitary étude in touch.

Swan Story

—After Baudelaire's "The Swan"

You said you would never fly away.
Above us a cerise sky—clouds like stroked,

pulled strands of hair, a ray of light angled
onto the surface of a green moving river

where we wanted to float like two swans.
I meant to write something else just now:

about three o'clock light. When you took off
I meant to write the ultimate Swan Poem.

But swans can't speak abandon or anything
else. They grunt-snort-whistle; are mute

with pointed beaks that pinch and poke
the ground. I have a card of a trumpeter

with an arrow pierced through its breast.
I pretend it's Baudelaire. He was sad too.

Swans don't drink or smoke; they glide
through currents. They move away,

come closer to shore and away again.
Like this three o'clock pewter light

that enters my window and flattens.
Then I remember flying in a storm.

The clouds turned awful-gray, my long neck
craned to understand, eyes blinking: *why?*

Baudelaire says it's okay to be sad
when you're just a swan.

You're a symbol of something bigger than yourself. You're on a river that moves you.

Remembrance of Things Past

—After Proust

The night Ben and I packed poems and rode to a cherry orchard
lit under a stormy summer sky, night sounds peeled as tangerines,

our bike pedals and chains creaking no, then yes, his breath over-
lapped with mine, was stolen, illicit. Laughing, we fell into a nook

enclosed by cherry trees blooming pink as the nipples Ben's wife
gave to her suckling twins at home. I told him about Simone de

Beauvoir, who, in an interview about love and her relationship to
Sartre (since neither believed in marriage) said: *absence is reliable.*

It's the outcome of every encounter, like birth gives life and a promise
of death. Love is the creation of absence. It starts as soon as we split

from the mother, and we spend our lives looking for her return
in the shape of someone else. I wanted to kiss him, but I could not

bear Ben's salty lips pressed against mine, the image of his wife's sweet,
milky breasts I tried to forget but couldn't, and yet I wanted to be

remembered so I let my head fall into the murky cove of his lap,
looked at him as if we would memorize this night because it would

end, and not be remembered for what it was, like the tiny white scars
speckled around his face weren't really scars but stars far beyond his head,

punctured into the sky. Truth is, his face erased into darkness
in a single stroke. We kissed like we forgot what we were doing.

In time he disappeared until one night pulled from sleep I stumbled
to a window, spied two cyclists speed past as the name *Ben!* startled

from my mouth—the sound like a dumb bat unleashed from a hole
in daylight, how it flits about, tree to tree, confused and completely alone

in a hunger it doesn't understand. Forgetting is night brought into day;
is the bat's stupor; is the woman the cyclists don't see at her window

looking not at them but for an answer to what her mother once said:
no one will save you. There is no better loneliness than a mother's love.

There are choices we make that aren't ours, Ben said, as he leaned into me:
so let's choose this, as Sartre would: like we're condemned to be free.

The Trouble With Flies

In my kitchen, next to the long,
sweet and sticky fly tape,
deep dried roots cling to kitchen
hooks, sanguine and purple peppers
dangle from green stems,
garlic heads grip tuberous roots,
some stray blanched threads loosen.
Remnants of the old garden.
This is—was—our world:
hung and hovering: how we
held each other ransom.
Today, out of nothing,
a tiny baby fly dives alone
toward one spot of
golden tape left, thinking,
this is where my family lives.
To watch her land, barely
new to the world of fake
nectar, to the idea of being
astonished, barely having
tasted filth, and to watch her
get stuck, to see her twitch,
wildly, then tear off one hind
wing, bits of her mouth,
and, near death, somehow
manage to break her body
apart and fly off on three
wings, leaving behind
a few filaments.

Mother Love

I entered the world and she wanted nothing
but to be rid of me. It's a kind of mourning,

like the atmosphere in Paris that turned from
sterling to oyster the day I leaned out her window

and watched the nearby market fill with vendors
selling fruit, vegetables, fish. I had never seen

the ocean, but the smell of salt rising from stands
filled my lungs with longing. I imagined the ocean

as wild and full of hate. By day's end, all was
dismantled, crates emptied, stacked, shreds left

to rot or scavenge. The homeless—some of them
mothers—gleaned scraps of fish head, parsley,

bruised tomatoes, shrimp bits—stuffing what
they could into plastic bags. I spit on their heads

like it was a form of speech. Most didn't notice,
but some looked up and shook their fists.

I was happy to be part of some other mother's
story besides the one my own refused to tell.

My mother rarely spoke. Mostly she studied
her face before a pink vanity that magnified

her silver eyes. Every day she plucked her brows
to a tense, drawn arc; pouted her lips into

a wounded look copied from French films.
I imitated her. Already I saw the world as full

of illusions. Outside her window the sky
glowered and gleamed like the ocean

she took me to see for the first time. I wanted
to swim but couldn't. A rip tide was close enough

to kill. So I joined a crowd that pointed to
a woman running into the waves to save

a stranded girl. We watched them fight
the current, whorls and funnels dragging

their bodies out. The girl was saved but
the tide turned, pulling the woman farther

out when the crowd gasped: *Oh no! It's her
mother*! And it was: it was the girl's mother.

We stood there, dumb, watched the woman
wave, bob, and drown. Then the sun came

back, turning every surface into a brightness
so blanched the air became the color of milk:

a thick, white silence, like nothing left to say,
nowhere else to go. Today, I am a room,

quiet as the table on which I write. There is
no ocean here. Outside my window is a broad

sky, a stand of birch that sways. Shafts of sun
float smoke that rises into leaves. *Am I alone?*

I hear a voice cry out a name, but it's not
for me. *Who wants to know?* There is a mother

somewhere, but we swim past each other,
toward the surface of things, as if to breathe.

In an Awning

When it is raining a body runs for cover
in an awning and finds another

who admits it has long longed for another
so a woman leans against a man

and their mouths slam dunk. A kiss
long and dumb under an awning

as great rains pour from a clouded night sky.
A body in an awning has no meaning

like the 23rd of May, but the pomegranate
he places in her hand the next day

is enough to recollect.
She peels it in front of him at a table.

They look at each other without speaking.

Between them lies a book about memory.
A chapter in it describes a mountain

we climb to see what we think we will
remember, as if from high enough

we can verify the past is still present,
only once there, it's too far.

Clouds mar the view. *Remember this*, she says,
handing him seeds from this strange fruit,

seeds that slide around their two solitary
tongues. Red juices bleed onto their fingers,

leaving stains inside the grooves of their skin.
That night they kissed, gutters flooded,

but if you pass by the awning today
you will notice an empty space.

At every moment of our lives we are
a frightful expression of ourselves.

Windows

It is March again. Blackbirds aim their starved orange beaks,
sneak worms from the earth, swallow them whole. I am told I am

no longer desirable. All around me buds edge into bloom.
I force a bouquet of calla lilies into a vase, snip the stems, aim their

white spathes toward the window. Something gathers at the base
and floats up. Is it the sun seducing the window? I watch each lily

open into abundance, think of Hercules carrying his son born
from another woman to Hera, another goddess he loved. He tried

to force her to milk his other son while she slept, but she woke,
pushed the baby away with such force her breast leaked and streaked

a path into the sky we call the Milky Way, splashing the earth
in left-over white dots resurrected as white lilies. Venus was jealous

of Calla, cursed her lilted beauty so she staked a yellow pistil
as the flower's center. I was young and living in Paris when my mother

told me this myth. My bedroom was bathed in sapphire,
an apology. I was told to stay out of the way: where light was reluctant

to enter. A small window faced a concrete wall. That spring,
I could only imagine everything rose and fell. In order to see more

I deserted my bedroom for my mother's blushed one,
where a half-moon window looked out onto a busy street. She was gone

in other bright vanishings, so I sprawled on her chaise longue,
tongue pink, prepared for long hours of gazing, attentive to every living

thing that drifted by on the street. I peeled oranges; ate cherries
and spit the pits out the screenless window. I thought I should stop:

I could strike someone on the head. I didn't. Below, at the corner
café painted scarlet the walls had an air of decay, and the windows,

covered in a mirror-like film, seemed on the verge of disintegration.
You could see through them, and, if you wanted, you could see yourself.

I discerned each passerby: would he look at himself, into the café,
in search of someone else? I studied women; how they reconstituted the parts

they took seriously in reflection--pale cheeks pinched to a rose blur;
lips shaded, smoothed to sultry. Always a desire to be seen, or ravished

by seeing--the thicket of beautiful--I entered it motionless.
One woman came every Wednesday. Before she entered the café,

she examined her face; raised and tweaked her brows into a snail's
arch, rubbed her forefingers over the contours of her cheeks and forehead

as if tracing circles on an aerial map, all the ruined lines. She readied
herself for the one inside. I could see his elbow on a corner table, cigarette

lifted, adored by his picked, cranberry lips. His hands were pale,
lupine fingers yielded and faithful to the ash. It was her face that seemed

shrewd. When she entered she looked around, though he always sat
in the same place. Maybe she was jealous of the other woman? Maybe

her throat went dry seeing him. Or did she leave children and
a husband at home? She seemed to want a thing more ripe, more true.

In winter, a snow fox fur almost strangled her neck; her red wool cap
pulled so low her eyes shadowed into somber fields. They barely touched;

mostly talked. But how they talked--it was seasonal. She leaned
into him, a willow, dangling layers she slinked off, one by one. Silver-blond

gush of hair; a pale clavicular song. Once, he reached and put his finger
at the base of her throat, traced a path down to her sternum, igniting her cheeks.

He listened as she spoke; got her coffee because it was specific.
I watched them savor the last sip at a distance. I embraced the window; the hours

I spent waiting to see them; this union. I did not know it was waiting
for me, later—the dull throb of each flowering season, the anticipation that runs

between living things. They never left together. She always went alone;
though before disappearing she stopped to circle her eyes in the mirror,

a rapacious revision of herself. In time I grew to want more than a café
door opening, closing, women fixing themselves to be more beautiful,

seasons evolving, winter melting its dead sexual urge into spring.
I would never know what was said between them. It all stayed inside.

The calla lilies are cut, leaves shaped to tongues alive by taste,
green stems stuffed in a vase set beside my window. Have I missed

something? The abundance of desire, that shadow in the window watching.

Acknowledgements:

My thanks goes to the editors of the following publications, where some of these poems first appeared, sometimes in different versions.

"Eve's Dilemma" *Aesthetica Creative Writing Anthology* — January 2018
"Greenland" "The Kitchen" "Bees" *Tinderbox Poetry Review* – March 2017
"Mother Love" "The Wedding Portrait." *Green Mountain Review* – March 2017
"The Cells" "An Old Woman Cooking Eggs" *Palaver Journal* – Fall 2016
"Sugar" *New England Review* 36.3 – 2015 (Nominated for Best New Poets 2016)
"Salt" Juked – September 2015
"A Natural History" *Shadowgraph 3* (2015) (Nominated for a Pushcart Prize, 2016)
"Refinement" *Naugatuck River Review* – Winter 2015
"The Trouble With Flies" Avatar Review #17 – Spring 2015
"Swan Song" Avatar Review #17 – Spring 2015
"The Destruction of Mother" *Hartskill Review* 1.3 – 2015
"The Bat Situation" *Hartskill Review* 1.3 – 2015

This book would not be possible without the world of people that helped shape it. Many artists and writers—some living, some dead—have left their unique imprint on the book's poems and its final form.

First off I want to thank the incomparable founder of Warren Wilson, Ellen Bryant Voigt, and the stellar faculty at Warren Wilson Program for Writers. Warren Wilson is an intensive and unique program that altered everything for me as a writer and artist. The faculty share so much of their experience with students in lectures, workshops and bookshops. I owe specific thanks to my mentors: Jennifer Grotz, Daisy Fried, Alan Shapiro, Rodney Jones, and Tony Hoagland. A very special shout-out goes to Connie Voisine who helped me organize the book, and who continues to mentor me long after my graduation. Unofficial mentors I feel gratitude for are Rick Barot, A. Van Jordan, Brenda Shaughnessy, Eleanor Wilner, and Kevin "Mc" Mcllvoy. Their particular support of complex lyric and narrative forms helped direct my work and the poems here.

Second, the poems in this book would not be what they are without the intentional, generous and meticulous attention of my own writing peers. Those I met at Warren Wilson go without compare in their art and friendship, but so do the artist-writers I met at the Vermont Studio Center, as well as the Loft Literary Center in Minneapolis. Our shared passion and attention for each other's work, and our enthusiasm to advance our craft has often buoyed me in times of despair and doubt. Many long phone calls, letters, and conversations kept—and keep me—writing.

A sincere thanks goes to the following friends for their keen writer's sensibility and the attention they give to writing and living beautifully: Lindsay Ahl, Nancy Allen, Brendan Basham, Tommye (Edie) Blount, Luke Brekke, Rachel Brownson, Stephanie Danler, Margaret Draft, Avra Elliott, Melissa Febos, Vievee Francis, Jennifer Funk, Jennifer Givhan, Lia Greenwell, Susan Greve, Suzanne Highland, Deborah Keenan, Eric Komosa, Caroline Mar, Nathan McClain, Kerrin McCadden, Kara Olson, Z.Z. Packer, Juliet Patterson, Adrienne Perry, Diana Sette, Somayeh Shams, Jessica Smith, Yerra Sugarman, Victor Valcik, and Tommy Zurhellen.

Third, I want to thank the anonymous thief who stole my computer at Spy House Café in Minneapolis one fateful day in January 2015. Along with my computer he pilfered a bag in which that morning I'd weirdly stuffed all my zip drives and notebooks. I'd planned to back up ten years of writing and print out all my poems that afternoon, which would be assembled into this book. When I reached out to writer peers and mentors to whom I'd sent drafts what I received through the mail became the order of the poems here. The uncanny outcome to loss surprised me, and for that reason I'd like to thank that little fucker for helping pare down what would have meant 150 pages of sifting. His theft ushered an unexpected change into my life, which is now a family motto:

Every loss is a detour, and detour inevitably leads to discovery.

Fourth, I am indebted to venerable institutions (Saint Catherine University's Annual Scholar and Writer's Retreat, the Vermont Studio Center, Warren Wilson, and the Loft Literary Center), and my supportive colleagues. I owe much to key individuals (Carl and the Scott family), as well as my extended surrogate family (Virgil Delegard, Amy Hilden, Ari Jensen). These folks helped care for my kid while I was away writing and making art. Without their support I would not have been able to focus.

Lastly, and most importantly, I want to thank my son Frank for being a free spirit, for his insistence that I keep making art, and that I tell all the truth but tell it slant.

With him everyday is a practice of joy.

Francine Conley is an artist who writes, and also performs. Her chapbook, *How Dumb the Stars* won the Parallel Press prize (2001). Since 2000 she has written, produced, performed and traveled dozens of multi-media one-woman shows in English, and she has performed collective collaborations with the traveling, Franco-American theater troupe she helped found, *Le Théâtre de la Chandelle Verte*. Chandelle traveled collaborative French and Francophone productions nationwide for fourteen years. After earning her MFA with a focus in Poetry from Warren Wilson in 2014, Francine helped found the Rabble Writers Collective along with five other women writers. She is the recipient of a Fulbright Grant to study Theater in Paris, and a two time Denny Prize winner for Creative Writing through Saint Catherine University. She's also been awarded residencies at the Vermont Studio Center, as well as the Breadloaf Writer's Conference. Individual poems appear in *American Literary Review, The Collagist, Green Mountains Review, The New England Review, Sky Island Journal, Tinderbox,* and elsewhere. For more on her arts: http://francineconley.com

CPSIA information can be obtained
at www.ICGtesting.com
Printed in the USA
FFHW010902221019
55628321-61456FF